SEVEN
BITES
FROM
A
RAISIN

SEVEN BITES FROM A RAISIN:

Proverbs from the Armenian

selected and translated by

Peter Manuelian

Aratsani Press

Seven Bites From a Raisin: Proverbs From the Armenian
© 2015 by Peter M. Manuelian

All rights reserved.
Published in the United States by Aratsani Press.

No part of this book may be reproduced in any manner whatsoever without prior written permission of the author, except in the case of brief quotations embodied in critical articles or reviews.

Proverbs translated from oral sources; G. Bayan's *Armenian Proverbs and Sayings*, Venice, 1889; and A. T. Ghanalanian's *Aratsani*, Yerevan, 1960.

Book and Cover design:

Vladimir Verano, Vertvolta Design + Press

ARATSANI PRESS
2752 Northeast 97th Street
Seattle, WA 98115

Author contact: pmanuelian@gmail.com

ISBN: 978-0-692-34569-6

To the memory of my parents,

Mardiros and Azniv,

and

To Carole,

Who hears the nightingale's song

&

The frogs' symphony

Eternity is in love with the productions of time.

~ William Blake

INTRODUCTION TO THE FIRST EDITION

From my earliest years I can remember proverbs and sayings being used at home. Bandied about as pointed barbs amongst the adults, they were also used as effective admonishments to us children. Of course, I didn't know at the time that they were "proverbs." They just seemed like natural utterances used to punctuate windfalls of talk and underscore weighty subjects, whether serious or humorous.

And when one was intoned in the rhythmic and lilting cadences of the Armenian and other Middle Eastern tongues, it put an end to whatever issue was at the fore—unless someone could come up with another to counter it. Human nature, it seemed to say, never changed and the judgments of centuries gone by were authority enough to assess the living present. Such language helped to locate life in a timeless and changeless medium, comforting to both children and adults alike.

When I heard, for example, someone acidly remark in the course of gossip that "No Peter or Paul will come from *that* house," I knew that the family in question was effectively damned. I recognized my name and had heard of an uncle somewhere named Paul, so I felt secure in the knowledge that whatever its presumed shortcomings at least my family couldn't have *that* said against them.

The passage of years has somewhat abated the use of traditional Armenian proverbs by Armenian-Americans. But for one primarily used to hearing contemporary English as spoken in the United States, it is always a pleasant surprise to realize that proverbs comprise an important part of the everyday conversation of people whose language retains meaningful ties to a traditional past that still exists in an ever-changing present.

The proverbs of Armenia we have before us shed light on a traditional agricultural society in which the sights and sounds of donkeys, mules, horses, goats, cows and hens figure prominently. The stolid donkey, its very bray the epitome of mindlessness, comes in for much chaffing. And the quintessence of asininity occurs when the owner searches for his donkey while sitting on it (p. 38).

Camels also appear on the horizon, providing to our western eyes a welcome departure from the usual beast of burden and reminding us that it is the Middle East speaking to us. A frequent destination for camel caravans crossing the Armenian plateau was Baghdad, in the hot Mesopotamian lowlands far to the south. Baghdad, glittering city of Harun al Rashid and the *Arabian Nights*, provides a cosmopolitan point of reference. The Tigris and the Euphrates, those famous rivers of antiquity having their source in the Armenian mountains, flow by the ancient city.

The traditional animals of folklore make their appearance here also: the fox, wolf, bear, eagle, snake, cat, mouse and lion—the latter still sighted at the turn of the 20th century along the southern boundaries of historic Armenia. But an infrequent foray into such literature is made by the partridge (p. 33); and the nightingale evokes the enchantment of the east (p. 49).

In several proverbs the Christian background of Armenia is evident. The donkey, after all, makes his pilgrimage to Jerusalem (p. 39), not Mecca. And what more solid and outstanding pillars of Christian society are there than Saints Peter and Paul (p. 1)?

However, the Armenian, whose concepts of nationality and religion often imperceptibly blend into each other, shows at times a worldly skepticism toward organized religion. Witness the proverb where seven priests baptize a boy and christen him Mary (p. 11). This skepticism is also directed towards anything organized, as in the following bit of advice: "Go home when the table is set and to church when the service is almost over (p. 12). Note that "almost," a rather Armenian gesture.

Often a healthy cynicism emerges, melding into a wise realism that is part of human nature, especially perhaps as it manifests in the Middle East. For example, the Armenian proverb "Ask God for as much as you like, but keep your spade in your hand" (p. 21) is echoed by the Arabic proverb "Trust in God, but tie your camel." And the fool tossing down the well a stone that forty wise men can't retrieve (p. 32) is a paradigm of countless Mulla Nasreddin tales common throughout the many cultures of the region.

In fact, many of these proverbs can be viewed as appropriate punch lines to the delightfully subtle stories of this wise fool. One can just hear Nasreddin say, "If I drown in a pond, it is the ocean to me" (p. 20) and picture him attempt to water a camel with a spoon (p. 35) or test to see if indeed one can start a fast with baklava in one's hand (p. 31). One of the more popular of these tales has Nasreddin first count his donkeys while standing in front of them, and then count them while seated on one, a tale similar to the proverb about searching for your donkey while sitting on it.

In translating these folk poems innumerable problems were encountered. The effect of many Armenian proverbs all too often

iii

depends on the rhyme and rhythm of the language. In Armenian, an inflected language, articles and prepositions are added on to verb endings allowing for a greater uniformity of rhyme and a greater brevity. Take, for example, the common proverb "A thief robbed another thief; God marveled at the sight" (p. 5). A version that would sound and feel like the Armenian might, if literally translated, read something as follows: thief thieved thief; God seed marved. But of course this would not do. For this reason several commonplace proverbs whose meaning and effect would be totally lost in translation have been omitted. Much of the punning that goes on in one language would be impossible to get across in another. What we have, nonetheless, is a representative sampling of Armenian proverbs, some from a previous age and no longer in wide use, but most still current for those more than comfortable with the Armenian language.

The proverbs in this brief collection were gleaned from a variety of sources, both oral and written. Acknowledgment is due to Garig Basmadjian who provided some choice examples in translation. Many have been translated from A. T. Ghanalanian's *Aratsani* published in Yerevan in 1960. No modern selection of Armenian proverbs is complete without reference to this definitive work of scholarship.

Peter Manuelian
Pittsfield, Massachusetts

Preface to the New Edition

OVER THE YEARS SINCE THE PUBLICATION of the first edition of *Seven Bites From a Raisin*, long out-of-print, several people have suggested to me that the collection would have been more intriguing if the original Armenian had been included. This new edition then, at long last, presents the proverbs with their Armenian versions. Its publication year coincides with the 100th anniversary of the Armenian genocide of 1915. On April 24th of that year, scores of prominent Armenian public figures, including poets, writers, other intellectuals, and perhaps even folklorists, were rounded up by the Ottoman Turkish authorities in Constantinople and sent to their deaths. It was a time, as one of the proverbs has it, when bread was dear, and death was cheap (p. 30).

With this new bilingual edition, readers of Armenian can compare the rhymes, rhythms, and assonances of the Armenian with those of the English translation, or just appreciate them on their own. Non-Armenian readers, on their part, may find it interesting to see the Armenian script, once archly described by Lord Byron in a letter to his friend, Hobhouse, as "….the 38 cursed scratches of Mesrob, the maker of alphabets….." (Byron, who spent the winter of 1816-1817 studying the language at the Armenian Catholic

Mekhitarist monastery on the island of San Lazzaro in Venice, elsewhere refers to it as a "Waterloo of an alphabet.")

This alphabet is presented here primarily in the words and syntax of Western Armenian, one of the two main dialects, the other being Eastern Armenian. The Western dialect was used in the Armenian provinces of the Ottoman Empire and points west. The arrival of the survivors of the 1915 genocide increased its presence in the northern Arab regions (Syria, Lebanon and Iraq) and in Europe and the Americas. The Eastern dialect was used in the regions influenced by the Persian Empire, east of the Ottoman, and is now primarily found in Armenia, Nagorno Karabagh, Georgia, and Iran, although recent immigrants have spread its use throughout the diaspora. The overwhelming majority of the proverbs in this collection are in Western Armenian. Occasionally an Eastern form or spelling occurs because of the varying oral sources.

Currently (2015) the Middle Eastern countries where many Armenians settled after being cleansed from their ancestral lands in 1915 are in tumult, chaos and war. Many Armenians have been forced to immigrate again. The vagaries of these contemporary events ironically comment on the many references in the proverbs to Baghdad, certainly no longer a destination to be sought. In a way, the Armenian language in general, and folk sayings in particular, provide a continuity for a culture whose vital presence in much of the modern Middle East has been sorely tested.

All but two or three of the proverbs from the first edition, published in 1980, are here. Included also is the original introduction, although I have corrected the page references for the proverbs mentioned in it. Besides the inclusion of the original Armenian in this new edition, there are a few changes: some of the initial translations have been edited to provide a better phrasing. But more importantly, the number of proverbs in the current edition has been increased by about 20%. In addition, I have added a few explanatory endnotes at the request of some non-Armenian readers. I've kept these notes to a minimum because I think the proverbs are better appreciated without much explication. The ambiguity of some of them is part of their folk charm.

I've been helped by several people during the course of putting this collection together. Acknowledgment is due to Artavazd Ginosian, Aram Khatchadourian and to Queenie Varjian for input on some translations; to Leo Manuelian for reminding me about the candle maker's son; Genevieve Lester for editorial suggestions; and to Carole Hooven for enhancing the flow of the English. However, any miscues in translation or other solecisms remain completely my responsibility.

I hope you enjoy your journey through this collection of 199 folk sayings.

Peter Manuelian
January 2015
Seattle, Washington

Seven Bites From a Raisin

Լաւ է մէկուն աչքը էլլայ քան թէ անունը։

Better to lose your eye than your good name.

Անվան գեղեցկութենը Վանեն – Բիդլիս, դեմքին քեղեցկութենը տրնեն բադնիս։

The beauty of a name is known from Van to Bitlis; the beauty of a face, from home to the baths.[1]

Աս տունեն Պողոս Պետրոս չէլլար։

No Peter or Paul will come from that house.

Թող խարիպը ողչ ըլլի, եօթը լերան եաին ըլլի։

Let a loved one be alive, though seven mountains away.

Կամուրջէն անցած ատեն որ որի դպեր է:

While we were crossing the bridge, our bottoms touched.[2]

Պարտոք խմողը՝ շուտ կը դարխրշնայ:

Whoever drinks on credit gets drunk faster.

Բախնիք մտնողը կը քրտնի:

Whoever enters the baths must sweat.

Փարչը՝ ջուրին ճամբան կէ կոտրի:

On the way to the well the jug breaks.

Հեռավոր սուրբը զօրավոր է:

The more distant a saint, the more powerful.

Մեղքը լալով՝ պարտքը տալով:

For sins you cry; for debts you pay.

Վերմակիդ համեմատ ոտքդ երկնցուր:

Stretch your foot as far as your blanket is long.

Որբը խնտայ նը որբ չըլիր:

An orphan who laughs can't be an orphan.

Վարտիկը վեր քաշել չի կրնար, ելեր Պաղտատ կը վազէ:

He can't even pull on his own underwear, and he's running off to Baghdad.

Հաւկիթին մէջ մազ կը փնտրէ:

He looks for hairs in an egg.

Վեր թքամ ունքս է, վարը մօրուքս:

If I spit downwards, my beard; upwards, my eyebrows.

Փակիր աչքերդ գիւղին մէջ որտեղ բոլորը կոյր են:

Shut your eyes in the village where everyone's blind.

Գողը գողէն գողցաւ, Աստուած տեսաւ զարմացաւ:

A thief robbed a thief; God marveled at the sight.

Ասեղով հոր կը փորէ:

A well is not dug with a needle.

Տասը հոգի ջուրը կը տանէ, ծարաւ ետ կը բերէ:

He can take ten people to the well and bring them back thirsty.

Առարգին երեսը թքեր են. թաթաւ կուգայ, ըսեր է:

Spit in the face of an ornery man, and he'll say it is dew.

Անջուր մի բոբիկանալ:

No water in the stream, no need to go barefoot.

Առաջ գետին անցկը գտիր,ետքը ջուր մտիր:

First find the ford, then cross the river.

Արապան կոտրի նէ, խրատ տուող շատ կըլլայ:

When the cart breaks down, advisors are plentiful.

Խօսք առ մէյ մը շարխոշէն, մէյ մը պզտիկէն:

Take advice from a drunkard — also from a child.

Տաղին ի՞նչ պետք է ուռի սանտր:

What good is a gold comb to a bald man?

Քորին ի՞նչ պետք է թէ ճրաքը թանկ է:

Why should a blind man care if lamp oil's expensive?

Բարեկամ չ'օգնող, թշնամի ինծի չվասող, երկուսը զույգ մը օղ:

A friend who doesn't help, an enemy who doesn't harm: a prized pair of earrings.

Նայէ որ իմաստուն ըլլաս, բայց տգէտ երեւնալ սորվիս:

See that you are wise, but learn how to appear ignorant.

Պզտիկ քուն կը քնանա, մեծ երազ կը տեսնա։

Short sleep, big dreams.

Գիտէ շատ երգեր, բայց ոչ թէ երգել։

He knows many songs, but not how to sing.

Շիտակ ասողը տեր չունի։

The truth-sayer has no master.

Ըսէ ճշմարտութիւնը բայց մէկ ոտքդասպանդակին մէջ պահէ։

Speak the truth, but have one foot in the stirrup.

Ծուր նստինք, շիտակ խոսինք:

Let's sit crooked, but speak straight.

Կը օգտագործէ մէկ տոննա պողպատ մէկ ասեղ սարգելու համար:

He uses a ton of steel to make a needle.

Ջուրը ջաղացքը տարեր է, չախչախը կը փնտրէ:

The flood's carried away the mill and he's looking for the miller.

Ծխնելույզը ծուռ է, բայց ծուխը կը բարձրանա ուղիղ:

The chimney's crooked, but the smoke rises straight.

Նոք չթրճած, ձուկ չի բռնուիր:

Without getting wet, you won't catch fish.

Անձրևոտ օրը շատերն ջուր կուտան հավերին:

On a rainy day many offer to water the chickens.

Երեսին կաշին հագնիս Պաղտատ երթաս, չի կտրրտիր:

If you wear shoes made from the skin of his face and walk all the way to Baghdad, they still won't wear out.

Ժամը շինվեց, մնաց գմփեթը:

The church is finished; only the dome remains.

Առանց խունկի մոմի եկեղեծի չըլլար:

There can be no church without incense or candle.

Յոթը քահանաներ մկրտեցին տղային, և դրին անունը Մարիամ:

Seven priests baptized a boy, and named him Mary. [3]

Մօրուքը եպիսկոպոսի, սիրտը հուլիանոսի:

Beard of a bishop, heart of an apostate.

Տէրտէրներ յոթը ստամոքս ունին:

Priests have seven stomachs.

Ոչ մոլլահի մուխ, ոչ ալ տէրտէրու ծուխ:

Neither the smoke of a mullah nor that of a priest.

Երուսաղէմ հասնք, քոր վարդապետի ձեռ պաչեցինք:

We reached Jerusalem and kissed the hand of a blind bishop.

Գնա տուն երբ սեղանը պատրաստ է, գնա եկեղեցի երբ պատարագը գրեթէ վերջացած է:

Go home when the table is set, and to church when the service is almost over.

Նոր եկա եկեղեցիէն, եւ դուն ինծի քարոզ կուտաս:

I've just come from church, and you're giving me a sermon.

Ոչ մէկը չասեր իր մածունը թթուած է:

No one calls his own yogurt sour.

Ամեն կլոր խնձոր չի:

Everything round isn't an apple.

Հավին դիմացը կորեկ կը ցանե:

He plants millet in front of the chicken coop.

Կերթա Երեւանեն բրինձ բերելու, կուգա որ ձավարը տնեն են տարեր:

He goes to Yerevan to buy rice, and returns to find his bulghur stolen.[4]

Ես խմեցի, դուն հարբար:

I did the drinking and you got drunk.

Ունքը շինելու տեղ, աչքն էլ հանեց:

Trying to smooth his eyebrows, he poked out his eye.

Մեկը չէ աղոթեր, չէ աղոթեր, աղոթեր՝ մատը աչքն է խոթեր:

When the man who never prayed finally did, he stuck his finger in his eye.

Մեկ փարճով հազար դուռ կանցնի:

In a single slipper he passes through a thousand doors.

Կամենալ կես ընել է:

To be willing is only half the task.

Մեկի մորուքը կրակ ընկել է, մեկել կասի, կեցիր՝ մուխս վառեմ:

If your beard were on fire, he'd light his cigarette on it.

Մորուքը համրեր են:

They know how many hairs are in his beard.

Մորը մանածը շուկան տարեր է:

He's taken his mother's weaving to the bazaar.

Ճահելի խելք՝ անջուր ջաղաց։

A youth's mind: mill without water.

Մոմճիին տղան կը պս՛ակես։

Are you holding a wedding for the candle maker's son?[5]

Մարդ մը որ կը վերցնէ մեծ քար մը չի պատրաստեր նետել։

A man who picks up a big stone doesn't intend to throw it.

Արիւն արիւնով չեն լուանալ։

Blood is not washed by blood.

Մեկ աչքն մեկալին չի հաւատար:

One eye doesn't believe the other.

Աչքերն չեն չհամաձայվի, նույնիսկ եթե քիթը չլիներ մեջտեղ:

The eyes would not disagree even if the nose were not between them.

Աղջիկը ոսկե օրորոցով հոր տունը չի նստի:

A girl with a golden cradle doesn't remain long in her father's house.

Մազը սրտիցն է ջուր խըմում:

Her hair drinks water from her heart.

Շատ անուշ է տակը բուշ է:

So sweet, but a thorn underneath.

Չհագած զգեստը կմաշվի:

A dress that is not worn wears itself out.

Քաշէ թելը և հազար կարկատաններ կնան ներքև:

Pull a thread and a thousand patches will fall off.

Մազէ շըվալին ապըշմէ կանթ:

A silken cord on a hair sack.

Սուրի կտրածը կ՚ադեկնա, լեզվի կտրածը չադեկնար:

What the sword cuts will heal; what the tongue cuts will not.

Ասեղը ու որ մտնէ դերձանը ետևէն կ՚երդայ:

Where the needle passes, the thread follows.

Աչքերը սրտին հայելին են:

The eyes are the mirror of the heart.

Տուն չունի, բայց դուռ կը փնտրէ:

He has no home, but he's looking for the door.

Բերաննին լեցուն է, փորերնին պարապ:

Mouth full, belly empty.

Ծովը իյնողը՝ ձեռքը փրփուրին կ'երկնցնէ:

A drowning man will grasp the foam.

Որ ջուրը զիս կը խղդէ, ես անոր ծով կրսեմ:

If I drown in a pond, it's an ocean to me.

Խոզի գլուխը խալիչի վրա չի կենալ:

A pig's head doesn't float.

Դէպի հովին թքնաս՝ երրսիդ կուզա:

Spit against the wind and you spit in your own face.

Ցանկացիր Աստծուց ինչ կուզես, բայց բահրդ միշտ ձեռքդ պահէ:

Ask God for as much as you like, but keep your spade in your hand.

Ողջ վարտիք չունէր, մահացած տաճար ունէր:

Alive, he had no underwear; dead, he had a temple over his grave.

Միշտ ըսէ ճշմարտութիւնը կատակի պէս:

Always tell the truth in the form of a joke.

Խեր որի խիեար եղաւ:

I did a good deed; it became a weed.[6]

Ինկած ծառը շատ փայտ է տալիս:

A fallen tree provides plenty of firewood.

Ինչ որ քամին կը բերէ իր հետը ետ կտանէ:

What the wind brings it will also take away.

Ծառ լինի՞ որ քամի չդպչի:

Is there a tree that isn't shaken by the wind?

Ամպի գոռալնու՛ գէորայ՝ անձրեւ չի գայ:

Clouds may thunder — and still not bring rain.

Արեգակը որ այլափ բարձր ու լուսաւոր է, մէկ փոքր ամպը կը ծածկէ:

The smallest cloud can hide the vast, bright sun.

Կրակը ձմռան վարդն է:

Fire is the rose of winter.

Կա՞րող է վարդը ծովը միջում, մանիշակը կրակին առջին դիմանալ:

Can a rose survive the sea or a violet the fire?

Սարին անհոտ ծաղիկն էլ իրան տեղը պարտեզի վարդի հետ չի փոխել։

A wildflower on the mountaintop would not change places with a rose in the garden.

Մեկ ծաղիկ գարուն չի բերեր։

One blossom doesn't make the spring.

Պտղատու ծառը գլուխը կախ կը գցի։

A tree heavy with fruit hangs its head low.

Ծառին ցած ճիւղէն՝ թութ չուտեր։

He won't eat mulberries from the lower branches.

Մէկ չամէչը եօթը տեղէ կը խազնէ։

He can get seven bites from a raisin.

Կամ աղը հոտեր է կամ մատաղը։

Either the salt is rotten or the meat.

Եփած կերակուրին վրայ պաղ ջուր չեն լեցներ։

Don't pour cold water on cooked food.

Թեփին տակ ձմերուկ չի հասունար։

A watermelon won't ripen in your armpit.

Չմերուկ կտրելով սիրտ չի հովանա:

The heart isn't cooled by eating a watermelon.

Մէկ ձեռքով երկու ձմերուկ չի բռնուիր:

You can't carry two watermelons in one hand.

Ով որ ասէ՛ մատս խիար է, աղը կառնի կը վազի:

If he'd say his thumb's a cucumber, you'd take the salt and run.[7]

Լսել է Պաղտատ խուրմա կայ, չի գիտեր ի՛նչպէս կուտեն:

He's heard there are dates in Baghdad, but he doesn't know how they're eaten.

Քացախը որքան զօրի ըլլի՝ իր կարասը կը ճեղքէ:

Strong vinegar cracks the crock.

Եթէ հաշվես սոխն ու սխտորը, ապա մի ուտեր կվեջը:

If you count the onions and garlic, don't eat the stew.

Սոխը շատ մի կեղուեր՝ կը բախի:

Keep on peeling an onion and it'll disappear.

Մեծպապան կուտէ անհաս խաղող, իսկ թոռը ակրաները կը չարդէ:

The grandfather eats unripe grapes, and the grandson grits his teeth.

Լիքը փորը չի կարող բան սովորիլ։

With a full stomach you can't learn anything.

Սէրը սխդոր է բուսեր։

Love has sprouted garlic.

Պաղտատ սխտոր ծեծեն՝ հոտ մեր քիթ պիտի առնի։

If they're crushing garlic in Baghdad, we'll smell it.

Հնդկաստան ընկուզ կոտրին՝ մեջեն կըլլէ։

They crack a walnut in Hindustan, he'll pop out of it.[8]

Տանձն ինձ, խնձորն ինձ, սերկեւիլն ալ սիրտը կուզի:

I have plenty of apples and pears, but my heart yearns for quince.⁹

Ամէն հաւկիթ երկու դեղնուց չունենար:

Every egg doesn't have two yolks.

Մեղրը հին փեթքին մէջ է:

Honey is found in the oldest hive.

Երբ մեղր ունիմ, Պաղտատի ճանճերը քիտեն:

When I have honey, the flies in Baghdad know about it.

Երբ հացը թանկ է, մահը աժան է:

When bread is dear, death is cheap.

Ուսըս ալիւրոտ տեսար՝ խորեցար որ չաղացպան եմ:

You saw flour on my shoulder and thought I was the miller.

Կեր քեզ ապուրը մեծ դգալով:

Eat bad soup with a big spoon.

Լականը վար ինկաւ չկոտրեց, ձէնը վեր ելաւ :

The pot fell and didn't break, but the noise was heard.

Փլավ եփողի ապուրը կեր, ապուր եփողի փլավը մի՛ ուտիլ:

Eat the soup of a pilaf maker, but not the pilaf of a soup maker.[10]

Բերանը ոսպ չթրջեր:

You don't soak lentils in your mouth.

Ձուկն ի ծովին՝ տապակը դնել ի կրակին:

The fish is in the sea, the pan's on the fire.

Գաթան ծոցը՝ պաք բռնել կ'ըլլայ:

Can you start a fast with baklava in your hand?[11]

Ինչ տեսել էինք տեսել, բոր հրրեշտակ չէինք տեսել:

We've seen a lot of things, but never a blind angel.

Խենթը քար մը ձգեց հորը՝ քառսուն ճարպիկ չկրցան հանել:

The fool dropped a stone in the well; forty clever men couldn't draw it out.

Խենթին սիրտը լեզուին վրայ է, խելացիին լեզուն՝ սրտին վրայ:

The heart of a fool is on his tongue; the tongue of a wise man in his heart.

Խելոքը մինչեւ խորհի, խենթը կամուրջ կ'անցնի:

While the cautious one ponders, the crazy one crosses the bridge.

Մէկին բառասուն օր խեւ կանչեր են՝ խենթեցեր է:

Call a man a fool for forty days, he'll become one.

Կագալին ըսին՝ ինչո՞ւ ոտքդ կարմիր է, - ըսաւ ձմրան ցուրտէն է, - քեզ ամառն ալ տեսանք, ըսին:

They asked the partridge: "Why are your feet red?" "From the winter cold," she answered. "Ah, but we've seen you in the summer, too."

Արծիւը իր փետուրներէն շինուած նետով կը վիրաւորուի:

The eagle is wounded by an arrow made of its own feathers.

Կանկառին ըսին՝ քու բունը ո՞ւր է. Ըսաւ՝ քամին:

They asked the bird where her nest was. "Ask the wind," she replied.

Քաղցած հաւը՝ երազը կուտ տեսնելով, թառը ոտքով փորելուն՝ վար կ՚իյնայ:

Dreaming of grain, the hen scratches the air and falls from her perch.

Աջովը գարի կուտայ, ձախովը հաւկիթ կը փնտռէ:

With one hand he feeds the hens, with the other he searches for eggs.

Կաղ էշով քարվան կը խառնվի:

He's off to the caravan with a lame donkey.

Ուղտ նստողը կուզեկուզ հան չի գա:

He who rides a camel doesn't become a hunchback.

Ուղտը կուլ կուտան, մժղուկը կը քամեն։

They swallow the camel whole, but mince the mosquito.

Ուխտը իր կուզը չի տեսներ։

The camel doesn't see his own hump.

Ուղտապանին բարեկամ եղողին դուռը մեծ պետք է։

The friend of a camel driver needs a large gate.

Ուղտը չեն ջրել դգալով։

You don't water a camel with a spoon.

Ուղտերը գացին պայտվելու, գորտերը բարձրացրին ոտքերը:

The camels went to be shod and the frogs lifted their feet.

Թեւը դարբնոցը չի գնալ:

The devil doesn't go to the blacksmith.

Սառած օձն տաքցրնես՝ առաջ քեզի կէ խայթէ:

Warm a frozen snake and it'll bite you first.

Օձին վրա թքնէ, օձը կը սատքի:

If he spits on a snake, it'll die.

Օձն ամեն տեղ ծուռ կը քալէ, իր բունը շիտակ:

The serpent moves deviously, save when it enters its nest.

Մէկ ծաղկէն օձը թոյն կը շինէ, մեղուն մեղր:

The snake distills its venom and the bee its honey from the same flower.

Ոսկի բեռով ջորուին արջին ամէն բերդի դռուռտիք բաց են:

A mule laden with gold is welcome at every castle.

Էշը ինկաւ գարու հորը, — ըսաւ՝ աս լաւ է քան մեր գոմը:

The donkey fell into a barley pit. "It's better here than in my stable," he brayed.[12]

Երբ ծաղիկներ տվին էշին վոր հնդրտա, էշը կերավ։

When they gave the donkey flowers to smell, he ate them.

Էշը ի՞նչ գիտի համը նուշին։

What does the donkey know about the taste of almonds?

Էշը եօթը տեսակ լող գիտէ, երբ ջուրը ինայ բոլորը կը մոռնայ։

The ass knows seven ways to swim; when he falls into the water, he forgets them all.

Էշը հեծեր, էշ կը փնտռէ։

He's looking for his donkey while sitting on it.

Էշը Երուսաղեմ քաճերէ քառասուն անգամ, բայց դեռ էշ է:

The ass has been to Jerusalem forty times, but he's still an ass.

Ձին եւ ջորին կը կռվին, բայց էշն կը կոխկրտուի:

The horse fights with the mule and the donkey gets trampled.

Ջորիին հարցրան՝ հերդ ո՞վ, աղ ասավ՝ մերս ձին ա:

When asked who his father was, the mule replied: "My mother is a horse."

Չի հեծնէ՝ Աստուած կը մոռնայ, ձիէն իջնայ՝ ձին կը մոռնայ:

When he rides a horse, he forgets God; when he dismounts, he forgets the horse.

Հեզ ձիուն կիցը սրտիկ կ'ըլլայ:

The kick of a meek horse hurts the most.

Շունի հետ ընկերացի, զաւազանդ ձեռիցդ մի ցցի:

Be friendly with the dog, but hold on to your staff.

Շաքարը շան բերաննէ:

The sugar's in the dog's jaws.

Շան սատկիրը մօտենայ, կ'երթայ ճեմիին դուռը կը պառկի:

A dog who feels death approaching lies in front of the church.

Շատ հաչան շունը ոչխարին գել կը բերի:

A dog who barks too often leads the wolf to the lamb.[13]

Երբ շունը կուզեն սպանել, կրսեն դէ խենդրձած է:

When they want to kill a dog, they say it's gone mad.

Շանը կաղութիւնը մինչեւ աղուեսի տեսութինն է:

The hound is lame until it sees the fox.

Խալիփի վրեն շուն կը հաչա, մեր վրեն կատու:

Dogs bark at others, cats at us.

Փրսկան ըսին փինդ դեղ է, տարավ խորունկ թաղեց։

They told the cat his vomit was valuable, so he buried it deep in the earth.

Քանի որ կատուին միս չի տրվին, կատուն ըսավ օրը ուրբաթ է։

Because the cat was given no meat, he said it was Friday.

Ձեռնոցներով կատուն մուկ չի բռներ։

A cat with gloves will catch no mice.

Մկան համար, չկա ավելի մեծ կենդանի քան կատուն։

To a mouse, there's no greater beast than a cat.

Երազին մէջ մուկը կարող է վախցնել կատուին։

In his dreams a mouse can frighten a cat.

Ջրաղացը կշահէ մկան միզուցէն։

A waterwheel profits from the piss of a mouse.

Մուկներըն ալ սալադա կուտեն։

Mice also eat salad.

Եթէ վազես երկու նապաստակի հետեվից, վոչմեկին չես բռներ։

If you run after two rabbits, you won't catch either.

Այծը կը նախրնտրէ մեկ այծի քան դէ մի երամակ ոչխարի։

The goat prefers one goat to a herd of sheep.

Եթե մորուքներ իմաստութիւն ունէին, ապա այծերը կ'ըլլային մարքարեներ։

If there were wisdom in beards, goats would be prophets.

Մեկ ոչխարին երկու կաշի չրլլար։

You can't skin two hides from one sheep.

Ոչխարին առջեւը խոտ ձգելուն պէս, դմակը կը նայի որ գէրացաւ։

Right after feeding the sheep, he wonders if its tail has fattened.

Փտտած յարդը առողջ եզի վնաս չի տար:

Rotten straw doesn't injure a healthy ox.

Եզը կը վերցնեն՝ տակը հորթ կը փնտրեն:

A calf is not found under an ox.

Կովին խոտ չտուածի՝ ձեռքը պտկին կը տանի:

He reaches for the udders before he's fed the cow.

Երբ նախիրը փոխեց ուղղութիւնը, որբալները դարձան դեկավարներ:

When the herd reversed direction, the lame became the leaders.

Աղուզը փուշին մէյմը կը նստի։

The fox sits but once on a thorn.

Գայլը թըղածը կ'ափսոսայ, հովիւը յափըշտակածը։

The wolf laments what it left behind, the shepherd what it took away.

Գայլին ձագը կրթելով գառնուկ չըլլար։

Train a wolf pup as much as you want, he still won't become a lamb.

Ամէն մարդու սրտին մէջ առիւծ է պարկած։

In everyone's heart there's a sleeping lion.

Առիւծը ճանճ չի բռներ։

The lion doesn't catch flies.

Մրջիւնը պզտիկ է՝ համա ասլանի ականջ է մտնում։

The tiny ant dares to enter the lion's ear.[14]

Ճանճը առիւծին ականջը կը մտնէ կը յաղթէ։

The lion is vanquished by a fly buzzing in his ear.

Առիւծը մեռաւ, բայց մորթը հոն է։

The lion is dead, but his hide remains.

Լավ որ ըլլաս մրջիւնի գլուխ քան դէ առիւծի պոչ:

Better to be an ant's head than a lion's tail.

Լուն ծռտէ, խապար կուտա:

A flea craps, he'll tell you about it.

Լվի մը համար վերմակը վառեց:

He burned his blanket because of a flea.

Գայթակղութիւնը գալիս է առանց հայտարարութիւնով:

Temptation arrives unannounced.

Սոխակը ոսկի վանդակ դրեր են, դարձեալ ախ հայրենիքը:

Even in a golden cage, the nightingale is homesick.

Թիթեռնիկը ծառն է ելեր, ինչ կա չիկա վար է թափեր:

A butterfly resting in a tree broke the branch.

Գորտին հարցուցին թի՝ ինչո՞ւ շարունակ կը պոռաս, — ըսավ՝ ձայնիս գմայլած եմ:

They asked a bullfrog: "Why do you continually croak?" He replied: "I'm enchanted with my voice."

Ամեն ծաղիկ իր տեսքն ունի, ամեն հասակ իր պետքն:

Every flower its beauty, every age its need.

Օրը կը լուսաբացվի առանց աքլորի:

The day will dawn even without the rooster.

Ականջիդ օղ ըլլան ըսածներս:

Wear my advice like a pair of earrings.

Մաղս մաղեր, ալիր մաղս կախեր եմ:

I've sifted my flour and hung up my sieve.

Endnotes

1. Some say "Tiflis," the capital of Georgia, instead of "Bitlis," a town less than 100 miles from Van, to give a wider geographical range. However, we might want assonance to trump geography in this case: the first letter of "Bitlis" is the same as the first letter of "baths" both in English and Armenian.

2. Said when two people are so distantly related that the connection on the family tree is not clear.

3. Several words for the clergy come up in the proverbs. Քահանա (kahana) is the Armenian word for a married priest; վարդապետ (vartabed) is a celibate priest; եպիսկոպոս (yehbisgobos) means bishop; and տէրտէր (derder) is a colloquial word for priest in general. Depending on the context, I may have used one for the other.

4. Bulghur is another spelling for bulgar, the popular cracked wheat product. In the hierarchy of Armenian grains, it is below the stature of rice.

5. Used when someone leaves too many unnecessary electric lights on (or candles in a past age), thus wasting energy and money. It was a question posed to me almost daily when I was a youth.

6. One example in these proverbs of the many rhymes and assonances that don't carry over to English well. The words խեր (kheyr, a positive thing) and խիեար (khiyar, a cucumber) are close in pronunciation. However, the words are not Armenian; they're borrowed from Arabic and Persian, perhaps because use of the formal Armenian words would not create the assonance. Borrowing from Turkish, Persian and Arabic is common, particularly in colloquial discourse, and in many cases the languages of the region share cognates. There are many examples of such usage throughout the proverbs.

7. Sometimes a bodily member other than the thumb is substituted.

8. Modern day India is Հնդկաստան (Hundgastan), but I've used the literal translation, "land of the Hindus."

9. Quince, not as common as apple or pear, has a subtle aroma and is sometimes placed whole as a sachet in a linen drawer.

10. Anyone can make soup, but the maker of pilaf, where each individual grain stands out, is a master—so they say.

11. The Armenian word for what's being held in your hand here is գաթա (katah), a kind of bread that's sweet like a cake. However, I've used baklava which is more universally known.

12. The common Armenian word for donkey is էշ (esh), which is close to ass in sound. I've sometimes used donkey, when the animal sense is more prominent, and other times ass, when it seems befitting to a person.

13. Depending on the speaker's accent or dialect, Armenian words for the same thing here may be spelled differently. For example, գել (kel) is a variant of the standard word for wolf, գայլ (kyle), which appears in subsequent proverbs.

14. Ասլան (Aslan) is Turkish for lion. The Armenian word առիւծ is used in the other "lion" proverbs.

A note on the meaning of Aratsani Press

When written in English, the Armenian word Aratsani has two meanings. The first (Արածանի) is the name of a river rising near Mount Ararat and flowing west to join the Euphrates near Palu and the villages of my ancestors. The second meaning (Առածանի) is "a collection of proverbs." Because of the two different letter Rs in Armenian (one regular, the other trilled), we have a nice double meaning in English, Aratsani.

About the Translator

PETER MANUELIAN has lived and travelled for many years in the Middle East, where he sweated in the baths of Tabriz and yearned for quince in Yerevan; saw hens fall from their perches in mountain villages, and heard donkeys bray in Jerusalem; cooled off with watermelon in the Ararat valley and ate the pilaf of soup makers on the shores of Lake Sevan. He once managed to get three bites from a raisin.

He has taught English at universities in Iran, Lebanon, Egypt, and Malaysia and at a seminary in Armenia. For many years he worked and taught at colleges in Seattle, where he now resides with his wife and 20-pound cat, who dreams of mice but has yet to catch one.

CPSIA information can be obtained
at www.ICGtesting.com
Printed in the USA
BVHW042020270120
570326BV00012B/661